How department stores are carried on

W B. Phillips

How Department Stores Are Carried On

BY

W. B. PHILLIPS

50334
5/7/01

NEW YORK
DODD, MEAD & COMPANY
1901

Contents.

INTRODUCTION.

No other branch of business can bear comparison with the wonderful results achieved by Department Stores, such a success as has made them the wonder of modern merchandising. These stores, that have grown to greatness from small beginnings, have a force and power behind them that commands general interest. Their store-keeping rests upon certain well-defined principles, and not upon chance, sensations or experiments.

It is not the intention in this volume to prejudice public opinion against Department Stores. No attempt has been made to enumerate any reasons why they exist and flourish, nor any effort made to prove that they are a necessity, or otherwise.

Whether they promote and build up the best interests of the people and country at large, or are detrimental to them, is a question on which intelligent opinion is largely divided.

The fact remains — a plain indisputable fact — that they do exist; that they have had a tremendous growth in recent years, both in Europe and America; that organizations of this character beginning a few years ago have developed into the largest and most successful mercantile institutions in the world.

The author, from several years' practical experience, having been closely identified with the policy adopted, and with all the detail of system employed, in running one of the largest Department Stores on this continent, having visited at different times the trade centers of America, and examined carefully into the systems employed in other stores of a similar character, and made careful comparisons, is satisfied that the enquiring public will appreciate the endeavor to give them an intelligent idea of "How Department Stores are carried on."

General Principles.

One of the great underlying principles of Modern Department Stores is cash. Buying and selling for cash. Cash and one price. Some deviations are made from this rule, according to existing conditions in different business centers; but this is exceptional, the larger percentage of trade being strictly cash, and this fact has contributed largely to the general success.

A few years ago nobody sold for cash. Nobody in those days marked the price on goods in plain figures and stuck to it. To-day this is done, and is acknowledged to be highly satisfactory.

The first aim is to get the best and choicest goods direct from the makers; and, second, to have the lowest prices, thus enlarging the purchasing power of every dollar. A Department Store is different from the ordinary store, by being big enough to deal in almost everything that people need; handling merchandise of every class that goes well together for all sorts of people; providing the means of doing everything quickly, easily, cheaply.

A store large enough to accommodate thousands of shoppers arranged to serve a purpose. Floor upon floor filled with merchandise, broad aisles, easy stairways, elevators to do the stair climbing, cash system for quick and easy change-making, with all the newest ideas in store mechanism; places to sit, wait, meet, lunch, talk and rest; in short, an ideal place to shop in. Everything done that can be done to study the convenience of customers and look after their interests. This constitutes one of the greatest factors in the success of modern retailing.

Looking after the customer. Looking after them in such a manner that the service is an attraction in itself, that shopping is made easy and comfortable. Service is what these stores are for. Complete service in every detail, beginning with the purchase of the goods, and ending with delivery to customers, guaranteeing every article sold to be exactly as represented, or cheerfully refunding the money.

The development of these great businesses is largely the product of better service, and this service has been effective in winning the favor of shoppers.

The strength of these organizations, while centered in well-known principles strictly adhered to, is backed up by a well-defined system of government, including all departments, and the development of this system has had a great deal to do with the success of present-day business. The principles referred to build up and support the business, but it is the careful management and perfect system which controls

The Management.

The central point around which the whole organization of Department Stores gather is the man, or men, who put up the capital; who own, control and manage the business; and who insist that the profits shall be consistent with their expectations. They not only put up the cash, but define the policy of the business, and organize and develop the system under which it operates. The organizing and executive ability, as well as the faculty of knowing men, must be largely displayed; knowing men, and how to combine them; knowing how to use their capabilities and energies, how to bring out all their qualifications and all their ambitions.

The management must be of large perspective and broad experience, make a close study of store-keeping ways and methods, be quick to take advantage of every new idea in service and appointments, and enterprising in everything that goes to make a business strong and successful. Associated with the head of the business, usually selected from active workers who live with the business every day, are a few who are taken into intimate relations with the business policy, and who very materially assist in its development, and in the working out and building up of the system by which the business is carried on. Capable, intelligent, energetic, lieutenants, who are intensely interested, and who exhibit no lack of earnestness or energy ; who are imbued with implicit faith and confidence in whatever may be advocated and decided upon, and who direct their best efforts to its accomplishment.

The System.

The system that dresses the windows with attractive goods, that provides the special bargains, that furnishes such a variety of goods comprising nearly everything that people wear or use, that gives a courteous and agreeable service under all conditions, that provides a place to rest when fatigued, that enables shopping to be done under such favorable circumstances, that delivers all purchases promptly, and if a mistake has been made in the selection, or for any reason goods bought are not satisfactory, presents no difficulty in their being exchanged or the money refunded; the system which does all this and more is not the result of accident or chance, but there is a vast machinery behind it all which directs and controls.

But the system must do much more than this It must provide for getting at results, and it is in this respect that the perfection of the system is reached. While the store space is divided up into little stores or departments, under different heads, who are given every possible leeway in the buying of goods and management of stocks, yet each head is made directly responsible for everything in connection with this part of the business. Each department is charged with the goods bought and with the expense of selling, and credited with the sales made. Each section pays its proper share of all general expenses, such as delivering goods, lighting, heating, elevator service, fixtures, rent, etc. The system employed enables the head of the business to always know the true condition of each section. It enables him to know, if desired, what each individual salesperson does; how much the total business is of any department on any day; what the expenses are for any given time; and these facts are not obtained spasmodically, but are regularly recorded and made use of. Lack of knowledge of the condition of any department does not exist. Success, or the lack of it, is apparent

13

at once.   The truth of Eternal Vigilance being the Price of Success is here acknowledged, and in no other business organization is more special care and attention paid to knowing constantly just what the actual results are.

Advertising.

Someone has said, "The time to advertise is all the time," and among modern business organizations none more thoroughly recognize and strictly adhere to this statement than Department Stores. Nowhere else is the science, the art, of advertising more intelligently understood, appreciated and applied. Advertising is recognized as the pulse of the business, the great vitalizing force. The importance of the relation of advertising to business cannot possibly be exaggerated, and for this reason it is considered most seriously. A recognized authority has said, " Advertising taken seriously in the retail business makes the policy of the business. It is the fundamental thing, the corner stone. Therefore, it demands the attention of the head of the business. I cannot think of any concern so large in its affairs, so extended in its ramifications, with so many responsibilities resting upon the head of the business, as to make the advertising subservient to the general management of the business, to make the head of the business ignore the advertising. The manager of a department, and the salespeople who are to sell the goods, should be told the policy of the head of the business so far as advertising is concerned, and the way the matter is to be presented to the public, so as to arouse the interest of all. It is important that the man at the head should vitalize the business by making everybody feel and know that the advertising, the address to the public, is made in conformity with his wishes, under his supervision, and is absolutely part of his plans for disposing of his merchandise. This being so, the proposition that the advertising of a well-ordered establishment makes the policy of the business is really correct.''

Many methods are made use of to present and keep the business before the public, but preëminently the best and most satisfactory is the newspaper. Its columns are recognized as the very best medium for business notices, going as it does into the homes of the people regularly, filled with the world's news, with information for everybody, about everything from everywhere. The newspaper column is the merchant's platform, his pulpit from which he speaks to the public. It gives his words thousands of tongues. It is in this way he reaches his audience and tells them about his goods and business. He must talk straight, and his address must be interesting and readable, and, above everything else, true. It must always have the true ring of honesty, and advertisements are becoming more truthful every day, as business men realize that it must be true or it will fail. People judge and form their estimate of a business by the honesty with which their advertisements are lived up to, soon find the truth-telling places, and trade gravitates that way with absolute certainty. Lying advertisements never built a permanent and successful business. Advertising of to-day is honest, or meant to be, and, every day, people are gaining more confidence in it, and are understanding more and more that it is a necessary and legitimate part of this business; in other words, a "Store Bulletin," to which they can refer as an honest statement of what the store has to offer them.

Advertising properly means attractive news, news of daily importance, news which is appreciated and taken advantage of by the most wide-awake, economical and thrifty. News that must not get old by repetition. There is nothing more important about the business than advertising. Of what use to have tons of merchandise to sell if the people are not told about it, told about it regularly? Keeping everlastingly at it. Hammering away day after day. Continuous effort in the right direction, systematic, persistent. The advertising must be clear, logical and convincing; containing exact and definite information, telling the store news plainly and honestly, telling the people what the store can do for them, telling it often and in the right way. Some departments may be systematized so fine that they don't require such undivided attention; but the advertising can't run along like this, but must have constant and careful thought. Every advertisement must have careful consideration. Carelessness or neglect will lead to serious results. Spasmodic advertising won't do. One might as well expect to close the store one day and open it the next. It must be regular, just as regular as the day comes.

Attractive advertising becomes a department of the paper, and people expect it — look for it with the same interest as other features. It is keeping the business prominently before the people and asking persistently for their trade that brings the business. Advertising is the greatest force, the most powerful lever, for facilitating business. There is a generally-accepted theory that advertising pays, but Department Stores prove by facts that the theory is true. There has been considerable talk about the uncertainty of advertising; but thoroughly understood and skillfully used in the interest of Department Stores, it has become a most powerful factor in contributing to their general success.

Back of Department Store success, are earnestness, persistence, concentration, energy; but between these and achievement stands advertising. "As the business grows and is prosperous, it is due to the controlling factors of system, merchandise and advertising, but advertising is the dynamic force which vitalizes all the rest."

With this understanding of the important relation of advertising to business, a decision is arrived at as to the amount of advertising appropriation the business demands, not a fixed amount — no more or no less — but about the amount expected to be spent, which depends upon the amount of business necessary to be done, and is determined by the percentage of profits. A selection is made of the best daily papers, space secured, and "The

Advertising Department " is ready for business. This department is under the direct management of the Advertising Manager, or "Ad.Writer." He has a distinct recognition as one having a separate profession, and must, if the best results are obtained, be confidentially taken into the inner workings of the firm. He must be familiar with the history of the business, its progress and development. While he may not require to know the exact amount of money made, yet he must know which departments are weak and which are strong. The strength of the best departments must be maintained and increased, and the weaker ones built up. He should know what the goods cost, where made, how bought, etc., and receive the hearty coöperation of the buyers, to obtain the necessary information to write up his appeal so as to secure a hearty response from the buying public. He must give an individuality to the store advertising, and see that every advertisement is backed up honestly, ever promise fulfilled, and that the information he gives the public is absolutely true. He must keep on file a complete record of all advertising, and should keep in constant touch with each department's daily sales, with a view to continual comparison with previous records. He must know what other stores are advertising and see that his prices do not run higher than competing figures. All window dressing, wagon cards, display cards and interior decorations should come under his supervision. He must decide the amount of newspaper space for each department; and though heads of departments may take issue with his decisions, yet, as head of the advertising, he does what he thinks is best, usually giving space according to the money-making abilities of the departments. He must understand the goods he is advertising, know all about their uses and superior qualities, go in amongst the salespeople and customers, and talk with them, in order to write convincing money-bringing, trade-building advertisements. Copy should be submitted by departments at least two days before advertisement appears, in order that he may give it proper attention, prepare the cuts used in illustrating, have his copy to the papers early, proof carefully read, and any corrections made. He must study the character of his illustrations, the display part of the advertisement, and having secured a distinctive cut or style of the firm name must stick to it, as it adds an individuality to the advertising. The type used must also be selected, usually good, clear and legible, easily read, but characteristic, so that it distinguishes his Ads. from all others, and advertisements should always appear in the same position on the same page, so that the public know just where to find them. He must not only look after all the detail connected with the advertising, but must be able to analyze the conditions which confront him, grasp every possibility of the field, be wide awake to every change, sensitive to every trade throb, and have such a command of the English language as will express his ideas in a captivating and original manner. He is the artist who, having the ability and talent, either inherent or acquired, paints the picture that attracts; and who, when backed up by good merchandise, right prices, perfect system and careful management, becomes a great business force and an indispensable adjunct to present-day business.

The Buying Organization.

A large force of experienced buyers are constantly employed, who visit the world's markets at regular intervals in search of new goods. The aim is to save all intermediate profit, by buying direct from the makers, making direct connection between the manufacturer and consumer, and thus getting as near as possible to the actual cost of production.

Hundreds of thousands of dollars are represented in the several stocks purchased. Assortments must be complete at all times, and there must be a constant income of new goods. As fast as one thing sells, another must take its place, and no interest must be overlooked in the buying. Buying in great quantities, they are enabled to send buyers regularly to the great manufacturing centers and leading sources of supply. Prices are low in proportion as orders are large, and ready cash secures the best trade discounts. To collect such a wealth of goods and have styles and qualities just right, means a good deal. It means that the whole range of merchandise must be known. To get the best in the world for the money, and keep assortments complete the season through, calls for careful calculation. The varied human needs of civilization are to be satisfied, and each buyer in his own particular lines must be a man of large experience, of most excellent judgment, and high mercantile ability. They must know the merchandise they buy, that such a factory has the best reputation for one line, that this mill excels in another class, never buying anything simply because it is cheap, but picking out the best manufactures in each department, always maintaining a strict standard of reliability; and that the goods are well bought is demonstrated by the persistent growth of the business. They buy to unusual advantage by reason of ready money and the great outlet for all classes of merchandise. Several of the largest stores render valuable assistance to their buyers by establishing permanent foreign buying offices, thus enabling them to keep in close touch with the newest styles and novelties; and from these offices the shipment of a considerable amount of foreign goods is managed, the service being so facilitated and systematized that a prompt and rapid delivery of goods is effected.

But the buyers' duties do not end with the purchase of goods. He is also manager of the department which is made up of the various lines he buys, and is responsible for the proper management of the same. In his absence while buying, he must provide a capable assistant to represent him and the department, one whose services are esteemed as second only to his own, and who, if need be, in many instances is quite capable of acting as buyer and manager in his stead. He is given almost complete control of everything pertaining to his department, must sell the goods he buys, and his permanent position depends entirely upon the success with which his department is handled. As "head of a department," he is expected to comply with the rules of the house and set an example to all those under him. He should be first in the department in the morning and last to leave in the evening. He should be thoroughly acquainted with all rules pertaining to employees, and any new instructions which may be issued from time to time, and see that they are carried out. He is expected to use his best efforts to aid salespeople in making sales, instruct inexperienced help how to handle and display goods, how to wait on customers, make out checks, and, in fact, see that all duties are intelligently understood. It is not sufficient that new, inexperienced help be given a number and salesbook and told to go ahead, but thorough instructions must be given as to the methods of doing business. In order that enquiries of customers may be intelligently answered, he should know the location of all the stocks of the house. If travelers' samples are to be examined, it should be done in the sample room provided for that purpose, and in forenoons only. Only in special cases is it permissible to examine samples in the afternoon, as he is expected to be in his department during the busy hours of every day, to watch the trade and see that customers are properly waited upon.

Certain expenses are almost wholly within the control of heads of departments, and must be watched by them with the greatest care. This is especially true as applied to the amount of help employed. By using care and judgment, it is often possible to do with less help, and thus reduce the cost of selling. This is largely supplemented by watching the sales of each salesperson, and enquiring carefully into any cases where there is a falling below the average percentage of cost.

He should see that all advertised goods are properly displayed at the counters, and that all the people in that section are promptly notified of all particulars, such as quantities to be sold, price, etc.

He should see that all slow-moving goods are reported promptly, and goods must not be allowed to get old, but be moved out quickly. Any goods that do not move readily *must* be got rid of — cleared out — whatever cash value they have must be secured, and at once, and no matter at what sacrifice; it being considered best to get what you can for them immediately, and replace the stock with something that will sell readily.

He should furnish a complete statement of stock to be purchased and hand the same to the office a reasonable time before going on a purchasing trip, and must have the sanction of the office to the same. Buyers are expected to respect the limits placed and not to exceed the figures sanctioned; but if the market is showing any special lots of goods which in his judgment should be bought, or he is confident that a saving will be effected on goods which are likely to rise in value by buying heavier, considerable latitude is permitted.

All business correspondence for the house should be handled through the regular correspondence office, be submitted for approval, and signed only by those authorized.

The buyer's work bears such important relations to the business, both in the selection of goods and in the direct management of his department, that his qualifications must be the best, in order to render such a service as is desired and demanded.

Receiving Goods.

A general receiving room for all case goods and packages is provided. Space is allotted to each department, and all goods bought must pass through this room before going into stock. Porters prepare all goods for examination, by removing lids of cases, opening packages, putting aside all paper, canvas, etc., which is held for reference until goods are checked, and goods are then placed in proper department space ready for the department managers. Heads of departments are usually notified each day of all goods to be marked off the following day, and furnished with invoices of the same. The receiving room is usually open for checking purposes from 8 A. M. to 10 A. M. only, and goods must not be checked off nor removed from this room during any other hour of the day, except by special permission. Goods are called off by assistants, checker compares with invoice, selling price and stock number are entered on goods, and selling price marked on invoice. Until properly marked off, no goods are allowed to be sent out of the receiving room. If goods do not come up to sample, and are to be returned, it must be done at once, and shipper advised. In case of errors or shortages, they must be certified to by two or three competent persons. All invoices should be returned to the office as soon as goods are marked off. Receiving room should be closed at 10 o'clock sharp, at which time all department managers and assistants should be back in the selling departments. Heavy goods, such as furniture, wall paper, etc., are received in their respective stock rooms and checked off in the same manner. Goods should never be received without an invoice.

Taking Care of Stock.

Salespersons must keep in good order all stock under their charge. Customers of the house, as well as those in authority, readily recognize who takes an interest in the business, by the display and arrangement of the stock. No excuse can be taken for merchandise that does not present a clean, attractive and presentable appearance. Every article should be properly marked or tagged, and each piece of goods ticketed in plain, neat figures, so that a glance will tell price, size, etc.

No matter what the stock is, it should be attractively displayed, and the display changed regularly, having a suitable card on all goods so exhibited. When a sale is completed and clerks are through showing goods, they should be replaced as soon as possible, thus avoiding confusion and keeping the selling space clear and in good shape for new business.

Serving Customers.

All customers should be waited upon with equal promptness and politeness, no matter whether the purchase is large or small, whether it is simply an enquiry or an exchange of goods. There should be no favorites among customers. First come, first served. A customer who is being served should never be left because a liberal buyer, who is well known, approaches the counter. Goods must not be misrepresented. Customers buy upon the understanding that they can get their money back without argument, therefore only true representation must be made. Exaggerated statements, or trickery in selling goods, is not permitted. In all matters relating to the business of the house the greatest courtesy is required. Clerks are expected to accommodate themselves, as far as possible, to the peculiarities of those they are serving, being civil and polite in their attentions. Should articles asked for be in another department, customers should be informed where they may be obtained ; and if clerks don't know, they should refer to the floor manager. If clerks don't happen to have just the article the customer asks for, they should show the nearest they have in stock, and if that won't answer the purpose, consult the head of the department, and possibly it could be procured. They should try and understand what the customer wishes and get it as near as possible, never showing too many goods at a time, as it is confusing and often results in the loss of a sale. If a second customer is waiting, a disengaged clerk should be called. If all are busy, customer should be asked to be seated until one is disengaged. The undue urging of merchandise upon customers is not countenanced, nor yet is indifference in the slightest degree permitted. While large sales are important factors with all salespeople, and largely form the basis for salary paid, yet genuine interest in their duties, the exercise of patience, showing goods pleasantly and cheerfully, polite attention and care in waiting upon customers, are also very important factors in the recognition of value of services. Clerks should always leave a good impression and never let customers go away feeling that they have been treated in an overbearing or uncivil manner, as it hurts the clerks personally and also the house. The interests of employer and employee being identical, better opportunity for advancement and greater compensation is assured the more the store prospers. Upon all matters, under all conditions, the greatest courtesy is insisted upon.

Exchanging Goods.

The general understanding existing with Department Stores concerning merchandise sold is, that if for any reason it is not satisfactory it may be returned and exchanged or money refunded, on customer's request. This understanding, however, has some qualifications,—such as articles that have been worn, when such a time has elapsed between the purchase and return as to render articles unsalable, goods made to order according to measurements, toilet goods, etc.; but, with few exceptions, the almost unalterable rule is to exchange cheerfully, to avoid unnecessary questions or remarks, rather preferring to be occasionally the subject of imposition than to leave an unpleasant impression. Where an exchange is desired in the same department as purchase was originally made, an exchange bill is issued. Should the customer select other goods of less value than the exchange bill, the cash office, when new

check and exchange bill are received,
will return the difference in change.
The exchange bill, when signed by the
head of a department, or one authorized, is good for its value in any department; and should the customer
not be able to make a suitable selection, this bill, when properly stamped
or signed, is good for cash on presen-
tation.   These exchanges, as collected
and audited, are usually deducted from
each department's daily sales.

Floor Managers and Ushers.

Floor managers must be thoroughly familiar with and see to the enforcement of the rules of the house, as applied to their sections. They must see that each department in their division is promptly prepared for business, covers off, and everything in order, and must have a general supervision over their division. Aisle space, circles and fixtures must be kept scrupulously clean. All cardboard, paper, twine, boxes, etc., removed from goods sold during the day, must be sent from the departments at regular intervals, and not allowed to accumulate and present an untidy appearance, being first thoroughly examined, to see that no goods are contained. Sweeping should be avoided as much as possible during the day, but the departments at all times must be neat and clean in appearance. They should not allow cash boys or parcel boys to loiter in their division, and should see that all customers are properly served, and

the greatest courtesy and politeness
shown them, whether buying or simply
looking at goods. Strangers from out
of town visiting the store should be
made to feel at home, and particular
attention paid them. Should they desire to be shown through the store, it
should be arranged. They should be
impressed with the manner of doing
business, and this effect is best secured
where consideration is shown them.
It is better to answer the inquiries of
customers by accompanying them to
the department asked for and requesting a salesperson to wait on them,
rather than pointing to that department, and much better to name the
salesperson than to use the word
" forward." They should see that
goods do not collect at any time at the
parcel desks, but that they are removed
by carriers promptly. They should
attend, in case of sickness or accident,
to any customer, see that they are taken
at once to the place provided, and report the same. Any claims or complaints of customers should be referred

to them, and their best efforts used to adjust any errors made, and, where necessary, refer them to the Complaint Department. They should see that customers returning goods for exchange, or desiring money returned, are promptly and properly served. They should bring to the notice of the house the existence of inefficient or inattentive help, and report anything which in their judgment should have attention.

Making Out Checks, Etc.

This is not as simple as it may appear, and to master it thoroughly requires time, care and attention. Whether it is filling out a purchasing ticket, a C. O. D. check, or a regular sales check, special care must be exercised, as one cannot afford to exhaust the patience of customers by exhibiting a lack of knowledge. Every check in a check book should be accounted for: a spoiled check should be marked "Nil" or "Void," be signed by one in authority and sent to the cashier. Quantity, goods and prices should always be written plainly, all blanks properly filled out, plain, neat writing, and particularly good figures. Salespeople are usually held responsible for all errors made in checks or on purchasing tickets, and should always use their own book. They should always mention to customer the amount of money received, and enter the amount on their check

at once. Many people strictly honest
might forget what money they handed
in, and when change is returned
might claim that the bill given was of
a larger denomination. Repeating
the amount received will avoid argument afterwards. Duplicates should
be closely examined, to see that the
black-leaf impression is good. Change
should be counted in giving it to customer, and where goods are to be sent,
the name and address given should
be repeated. The use of purchasing
tickets should be encouraged. Customers should be asked if they intend
making further purchases, and the
use of purchasing ticket suggested.
The delay in settling for each purchase is thus avoided and customers' time is saved, as they can pay
for all purchases at once. Salespersons should see that their department
letter is on their check book. Check
books should commence with No. 1
and run consecutively to the end, and
should be examined to see that none
are missing, and checks should never

be altered. All checks should be sent to the cash office immediately upon being made out

Inspecting, Checking and Parcelling Goods.

Parcel desks are usually conveniently located at all counters, for the purpose of examining and wrapping goods sold. All goods sold, whether taken by customers or sent by the delivery, should first pass through the parcel desk. Goods sold should be passed to the parcel desk by the salesperson with the bill, and they should always be examined carefully, to see that they correspond. Price, quantity, number of yards, etc., should be checked and goods should be examined, to insure their being in perfect condition, not cracked, soiled, or injured in any way. Should goods when compared with bill be found short or over, marked wrong, or not satisfactory in any way, they should be returned to the salesperson at once, with refusal to parcel goods until everything is O. K. Parcels should not be given to customers, but handed back to the salesperson direct. Every

46

taken parcel should have the sales number marked on the outside. When parcels are to be sent, the address should be on the bill and also on the address slip, and they should always compare. Care should be exercised in handling goods likely to be soiled, crushed, broken or damaged. Where necessary, they should be put in boxes or sent to be specially packed. Every parcel should be securely and properly wrapped, using no more paper or twine than is necessary. Goods to be sent should not be held at the desk, and if carriers delay unnecessarily in calling, the matter should be reported to the head of the department or floor manager. Attention should be paid to the order in which parcels are handed up, so that customers will receive their purchases in the order in which they have been served. All desk supplies, such as paper, bags, twine, purchasing tickets, etc., should be obtained in the morning, at which time the stock-supply room should be open.

Collecting Goods for Delivery.

Goods to be delivered are usually divided into two classes, individual purchases styled "Sent Parcels," and collective purchases made on purchasing tickets. Checks for sent parcels when made out in salesperson's check book in duplicate, with name and address slip and hour of delivery, should be separated, one half going to the cash office with the cash received, and the other half going with the goods.

Checks made out for purchases on purchasing tickets are usually different in color from ordinary sales checks, and are attached to purchasing tickets. As made out by salespersons in duplicate, one half is detached with address and sent with the goods, and the other half remains attached to the purchasing ticket until the purchase is completed. Goods sold are immediately wrapped, carriers call and goods are delivered through slides, elevators, etc., direct to the shipping-room floors. Sent parcels are separated from others and address label attached. Goods bought on purchasing ticket are placed in compartments whose number corresponds with the number on checks received with goods. As customers finish buying, they visit the pay office, where cards are handed in, totalled, cash paid, instructions as to delivery entered on the card, which is handed to the sorting section. Goods are here checked with card, to see that they correspond by number and amount, the address is carefully examined, when parcels are wrapped and passed to the delivery section, where they are assorted as to routes, entered on drivers' sheets by name, address, number of parcels, and checked off when given to drivers. Salespeople are always kept informed as to the regular hours of deliveries, and signal bells are usually rung notifying each department before each delivery closes. No parcels should be promised for that delivery after the bell rings, and all goods to be sent by that delivery

49

should be in the delivery room a few minutes after the bell rings. All arrangements for special deliveries should be made at the pay office, and all parcels should go by the delivery marked. if received on time.

Delivering Goods.

Drivers should know their routes thoroughly, so as to deliver with as much despatch as possible. When delivering, they should wear uniforms (a portion of the expense of which is usually paid by the house). They should be kept neat and clean, and when repairing is needed it should be done promptly.

Drivers are usually held responsible for damages or breakages, resulting through carelessness or neglect, either to goods or rig, and must account for horse covers, blankets, rugs, etc., with which they may be supplied. Drivers should always weight their horses when leaving the wagon. Each driver should be given sufficient money for making change, which he must have with him on each delivery for C. O. D. parcels, and excuses, as a rule, are not accepted for the non-delivery of a parcel on account of inability to make change.

Drivers should not allow C. O. D.

parcels to be opened without an order. Customers should be told that this rule cannot be broken; but if they pay for goods that are not satisfactory they can be returned and the money will be refunded. Drivers are held responsible for all parcels entered on their sheets, and should check off these parcels at the store, placing them in the wagon in the order of delivery as near as possible, thus saving time in sorting up their loads while on the route. Amounts due on C. O. D. parcels should be compared with entry on C. O. D. sheets, to avoid mistakes. When the delivery is completed, sheets should be signed and returned, and if, for any reason, any parcels have not been delivered, satisfactory explanations should be given. Any repairs needed should be reported upon arrival at the stables. Notes should be made of any complaints from customers and the same reported. When instructions are given to call for customer's goods, they should be got at the first opportunity and handed over to the proper person. If not able to obtain them, the reason should be given. Under no circumstances should passengers be carried while delivering goods. Special instructions are usually issued for extra deliveries before holidays, or on extra busy days.

Stables.

The stables are usually models of neatness and perfect in arrangements, every modern convenience being brought into use, providing accommodation for a delivery system of hundreds of horses and wagons used daily in delivering goods in the city and suburbs. Heated throughout with steam, lighted by electricity, and electric power applied to rotary brushes for grooming, hydraulic elevator service capable of lifting tons of feed and grain to upper floors, basement fitted up with complete blacksmith shop for horse shoeing, wagon and sleigh repairing. Ground floor space is usually devoted to wagons, each having its respective station. Easy stairways provided for horses to reach the upper floors, which are constructed to bear almost unlimited weight, divided into rows of stalls with aisle space between. Harness rooms, cleaning rooms, harness repair shop, hospital for sick horses, paint room, etc., together with the most modern machinery for grinding and chopping feed.

The stables must always be kept clean and well ventilated. Horses must never be taken out without being fed, watered, cleaned and properly shod: a lame or sick horse should never be used.

Harness should be washed and cleaned regularly, wagons oiled, tightened up and kept clean. Nothing should be allowed to leave the stables except in first-class condition. All repairs should be attended to at once. Wagons should be at the store in time for all deliveries. A record should be kept of the men's time and sent to the office regularly. Drivers' and stablemen's wages should be obtained on pay day; the pay roll should be signed by each one, and returned to the office. All C. O. D. money received from drivers at night should be put in sealed envelopes and placed in safe keeping.

A watch should be kept in the

stables at night, and a regular patrol made to see that all horses are properly fastened, blankets on and everything in good shape. Wagons should be washed at night and wagon signs thoroughly cleaned. All wagons should be examined carefully, and a written report handed in of all repairs needed, together with wagon number. All fire pails, hose and appliances to be used in the event of fire should be examined regularly, to see that they are all in good working order.

General Cash Office.

A central cash office is established for receiving all receipts from sales made, and arranged for quick and easy change-making. As a customer makes a purchase, a duplicate of the check or bill made out for the same, together with money received from customer, are sent direct to the cash office, the most improved method being by pneumatic cash carriers. As received, checks are placed on file and any change returned to clerk. Thus the totals of checks and receipts of each cashier's desk must agree. Each cashier makes up a report of the amount of cash received, and cash is given head cashier, who recounts it. The checks of each cashier are kept separate and sent to the auditing office, where they are totalled, and this total must agree with the amount of cash in the head cashier's hands, and correspond with the amount on cashier's report.

Check Office, or Auditing Department.

This department should make up the total receipts of each cashier by the sales checks received, compare them with cashier's report, and re-check until they are found correct. It should also make up each department's sales, arrange each salesperson's checks into original book form by number, and report any missing checks, auditing all checks and reporting any errors. The work of obtaining the different totals required is greatly facilitated by the use of adding machines, which insure both accuracy and despatch.

This auditing of checks thus provides a positive check upon the amount of cash received by each individual cashier, furnishes an accurate account of the exact amount of business done by each department, and the total daily business done by the house, besides showing the exact amount of goods sold by each indi-

vidual salesperson, which may be made
use of to estimate their value as compared with each other, and largely
governs the individual wages paid.

C. O. D. Business.

Large amounts are represented in the business as sold and paid for, cash on delivery, and, therefore, this branch is given special attention. Special C. O. D. books are furnished every department, and such special care exercised in recording the amount to be paid, address, etc., as will prevent any errors or misunderstandings. All C. O. D. parcels are entered upon special sheets or books provided drivers, and are checked off as paid in by drivers at the C. O. D. office with the record kept there, which should show the customer's name and address, department that goods were bought in, who sold them, the amount of the C. O. D., the date and amount paid.

Where goods are sent to distant towns, and considerable time must elapse before returns can be made, these outstanding C. O. D.'s must be watched closely, checked up regularly; and in the event of any unnecessary delay corresponded about, and such knowledge obtained as will furnish accurate information about each individual account.

The Mail-Order Business.

The mail-order trade as associated
with Department Stores began in a
very small way : it began with a few
requests from customers out of town
asking for samples and prices of certain goods, a few letters of enquiry
regarding one thing and another.
These requests and enquiries, properly
answered, brought in the first orders,
which were carefully filled to the satisfaction of the customers. They
told their friends about it, and more
enquiries were answered, more orders
received. This encouraged some effort, and special circulars or booklets
were issued telling about the store and
goods. These were mailed to regular
customers, and a few thousand extra
sent to carefully-selected names of
possible customers, until gradually
extra help was required to attend to
these orders, to answer the correspondence, etc. ; and it was found necessary to systematize this branch of the
work, to organize and establish a

"Mail-Order Department." The mail-order trade grew up side by side with the store trade. When the store was young and variety of goods small, the mail-order trade was limited; but as the store grew, as extra space was needed for increased service, and new goods and new departments were rapidly added, the mail-order trade increased in proportion, keeping abreast of it all the time.

Mail-order customers could not know but very little about the house they dealt with except through advertisements, or from hearsay, and, therefore, the reputation of the business depended upon the goods sent and the treatment they received. The foundation of this business was well laid from the beginning. The principles inculcated were that a clear understanding must exist between the house and the customers — that goods would not be misrepresented, that customers would be told in plain words what they were, and that they would be found to be exactly as represented, or that their money would be refunded; and that's what they wanted.

The management and method were perfected, and the resposibility of handling the business fully recognized, and an honest endeavor made to satisfy every reasonable demand. They realized that it is one thing to create a business of this kind, and another thing to retain it; that it costs more to get a new customer than to retain one already secured. Anything, therefore, that would destroy the confidence of a customer in the house or leave an impression that would tend to injure trade must be strongly condemned, and to strengthen this position a personal interest in every order was encouraged and insisted upon. Mail-order buyers must learn to interpret the customers' wants, and see that the detail of every order is carefully attended to. The correspondence must contain the fullest explanations; the goods must always be properly checked, packed and shipped;

and every head of every department must take a lively interest in this work, and impart that interest to the sales-people; and only so far as this personal interest extends, from cash boy to president, does the business prosper.

Upon this foundation has been raised a business of such proportions that it scarcely knows any limits, and wherever telephone or telegraph, mail or express, reaches, there you will find this business represented. Distance makes no difference. Customers served at any time and in any place. Catalogues, representative of the entire stocks of these large houses, are issued from time to time, and regularly find their way into the people's homes, no expense being spared to keep customers informed regarding goods and prices. The methods employed have won their trade, and fair treatment retains it. The tremendous growth of this business is the most satisfactory proof that it has succeeded. It clearly demonstrates that they have the confidence of their customers everywhere, that buying in this way is becoming better understood and appreciated; and that the method of shopping by mail is no longer an experiment, but, beyond argument, is an acknowledged success. A perfectly organized mail-order department is a distributing agency for the whole country, requiring a perfect system, demanding intelligence, exactitude, and promptness, carefulness in filling, and despatch in sending orders.

It reaches out for the trade of people in distant towns and villages. These places are full of bright, intelligent people, whose ability to buy is unquestioned. They are reached only by intelligent and truthful advertising. The mails take the counters of the big stores to the doors of these people. They like to shop by mail. They like to get samples and catalogues, and to make a selection of city goods, being strongly impressed that they get something different from what the local dealer supplies; something their neighbors haven't got, something stylish, exclusive. The means of communication are better and quicker than ever before. Whoever can write a letter can send for nearly everything they want. Wherever the catalogue goes the store goes.

Some of the appeals made, statements advanced, and arguments used to influence and encourage trade among out-of-town customers might be classified as follows:

Whenever you order, always bear this in mind, that if you don't get goods as represented, back goes your money to you as soon as you want it.

The smallest order you send will receive the same prompt and careful attention as if it were ever so large.

Where you and your neighbors order together, goods can be packed separately and forwarded in one shipment, thus making the charges low.

Selling goods at fair prices every day should interest you.

It may be a satisfaction to select goods yourself, but your orders by mail will be promptly and faithfully executed.

Out-of-town customers always get the benefit of any reduction in the price of goods.

Freight is a small item where customers are saved many times the cost of transportation.

You are at absolutely no risk whatever in ordering by mail, as you always get the best and pay the least.

Samples and prices are sent free of charge, therefore there need be no hesitation in asking for them.

A trial order will convince you that it will be filled carefully and promptly.

If goods are not all right, you don't have to keep them.

The goods offered are bought for cash in large quantities, sold direct to customers for cash and not through agents, therefore the traveling man's salary and expenses, the middleman's profits, his losses and poor accounts, are not paid by you.

Mistakes are rarely made; but always rectified.

Where there is the slightest cause for complaint, if you write fully, everything will always promptly be made right.

The bigger saving is made on the bigger order you send.

No charge is made for packing goods, and they always open up in first-class condition.

Your money is refunded every time if you are not satisfied. Goods are bought direct from the manufacturer, and then go direct to you.

Your smallest order will be filled at the same price as the customer who buys a thousand dollars worth. Goods marked at one price only.

Isn't it much more satisfactory and much easier to sit down at home, look over the catalogue, select the goods required and mail your order, than to depend upon stores where the stock is small as well as assortments incomplete, and get something that does not give you half satisfaction, notwithstanding that you do pay an extravagant price?

If an error is made, and it's not your fault, you are not asked to pay any expense incurred.

Some of the most successful men of the day give you in the catalogue sent the benefit of their thought, experience and hard work.

It may be a surprise to compare catalogue prices with others, but always a favorable one for the catalogue.

Confidence in the goods offered at the prices asked was established long ago.

The man is prosperous who saves a dollar on this and a half dollar on that: the prices quoted help you in this direction.

The goods offered are *exceptional*, on account of the price; and *rare*, because of their exclusive style.

Honest value is guaranteed for every cent you send, or it is sent back again.

It pays you to deal where no false representations are made, but where goods are sold exactly as advertised.

The goods offered are honest, the prices are right, customers are everyday honest people ; and that's why it's easy to do business together.

You don't save the freight when you buy at home ; the freight and a big profit as well are added in the price.

The whole truth of the matter is — *what promises are made, are kept.*

It is the belief engendered in the truth of these and other statements, the influence they exert in convincing, and the persistent method of keeping it up, that attracts this particular trade ; and the faithfulness with which all promises are kept, all obligations fulfilled, that builds the business up on the lines of perfect confidence and retains it.

All may not be agreed upon the effect the response to this method of doing business has upon the country at large ; but it is, nevertheless, a fact that the people everywhere are giving their material support to houses whose advocated policy is to supply them everything on which they can save them money, and it has proved to be a pronounced success to the promoters.

The possibilities of increased trade through the medium of the mail-order department appear almost unlimited. The amount of business that may be done has evidently never yet been measured, and no other branch of the business is apparently as capable of as large development as the mail-order trade.

Catalogues.

The general catalogue of Department Stores stands in the same relation to the mail-order trade as the newspaper does to the store trade. It is the chief medium for mail-order advertising. Though supplemented in various ways by special advertising, yet the catalogue stands distinctly alone as the indispensable means for securing and retaining the trade of out-of-town customers; and bearing this important relation to the business, extraordinary care is exercised in its preparation from start to finish. It is the silent traveler, the individual salesman; and as the highly successful representative salesman must have qualifications that bring business, so the catalogue must have the essentials which will insure successful results. These consist of appearance, paper, printing, illustration, arrangement, description, goods, prices, etc.; all of which must be thoroughly understood and intelligently carried out, not only in the relations they bear to each other, but also in the relations they all bear to the general effect and result.

The quantity to be issued is first decided, depending upon the number of present customers to be provided for, and the additional quantity required for extra circulation to influence new trade, which increase depends upon the amount of new business likely to be done, and the appropriation for which is usually determined upon a percentage of the profits. Next in order for consideration, is the size of the catalogue. The number of pages varies slightly, according as it is a spring or fall issue, and any increase from previous issues is governed by the addition of new stocks into the business. If new departments have been added, additional space must be made in the catalogue to provide for them. The paper is next selected. The size of the sheet must be accurately determined and the weight fixed, having due reference to the weight of the book when completed, as the postage for mailing is an important factor in the cost, and an extra ounce over weight might mean a great additional expense. The inside paper should be light but strong, and of such a color and finish as to produce the best effect with whatever character of cuts are used in illustrating. Particular attention must be paid to the cover paper, it must be of suitable weight and color and of a high finish, capable of producing a superior cut in colors, and extra strong, in order to stand handling. Tons of paper are required for the issue of a catalogue, which is usually bought direct from the mills, being manufactured expressly to order as to size, quality and finish specified, and delivered as required.

The cover design must be decided upon early, giving the artist time to fully complete his drawing, and the engraver time to execute his best work. It must also pass through experimental stages with the printer, possibly proving in a variety of colors, criticising and comparing, until the best effect is secured and selection is made ; and to do this and work off thousands of covers, and have each one perfect, the work must not be hurried. The cover design must be good, both front and back. It should interest and attract, and at first glance create a favorable impression. It should be a quick-acting advertisement, characteristic of the business, telling the reader instantly what it is about, so distinctly individual and striking that it insures attention like a flash. A good cover design is a most important feature of any catalogue, requiring originality of conception and the best artistic engraving and printing skill in its execution. Such a cover is always worth infinitely more than it costs.

Arrangements are next made with engraving companies whose artists and engravers are to prepare the drawings and provide the cuts used in illustrating the catalogue, and whose abilities and resources are sometimes taxed severely to get the work out as required.

The quantity to be issued and the size of the book being determined, paper selected, and artists and engravers secured, the work of compiling the catalogue begins. General catalogues are issued semi-annually, usually in March and September. A definite date is fixed when the catalogue is to be completed, and everyone associated with it in any way must work to that end; not always easily accomplished, but possible, and therefore insisted upon. Blank books are usually provided heads of departments, who are expected to use them, thus preserving a uniformity in the preparation of copy, and facilitating the work of the catalogue manager and printer. For months previous to the issue of the catalogue the buyers have been securing goods from everywhere, planning ahead, anticipating the wants of customers by making extensive preparations for the future. The world's markets must be visited and examined into, finding out what is new in this line, what change in that, whether this new idea in lamp goods is what the people will want, what designs in baby carriages are new and attractive, whether this style of boys' clothing is correct or not, knowing the latest ideas in gloves, laces, ribbons, handkerchiefs, fancy goods, etc.; securing the newest and most fashionable dress fabrics, knowing what styles in millinery, jackets, mantles, blouses, wrappers, etc., will prevail; seeking out, buying and arranging for quantities and deliveries to meet the demands of the trade — in fact, going over the whole range of merchandise.

The department manager's selections from these goods, as to quality, variety and price, must be carefully made, keeping in view the character of the trade appealed to and being governed in this by his experience and knowledge of its requirements.

His descriptions must be accurate and
short, but comprehensive, telling exactly what the goods are, giving the
facts in a clear, truthful and intelligent
manner. He must illustrate his goods
where possible, the better to enable
the customer to form an opinion as to
the shape, style, appearance, etc.
Valuable assistance is rendered heads
of departments in this particular by
the catalogue manager, who, by reason
of his work, has made careful comparison of other catalogues, and has
kept in constant touch with everything
new in the way of illustrating, and is,
therefore, ready with ideas and suggestions, which are utilized to the best
advantage. Goods to be illustrated
are set aside, the artist is given full
instructions as to what is desired,
style and size of cut required, group-
ing of articles or figures, etc., and the
work is put in hand. Drawings are
submitted to catalogue manager, who
with head of department examines the
work, suggests the necessary changes,
criticises carefully, points out any de-

fects, and, when satisfactory, passes them. Each drawing must be examined minutely. The pose of this figure, the artistic arrangement of this group of figures, whether the arm is too short or too long, or any part out of proper proportion; the way this skirt hangs, and the effect that fold produces, the completeness and accuracy with which the detail of trimming is shown; whether this hat or bonnet should be shown with front, side, or back view, the faces to be baby-like, youthful, or otherwise, thus indicating who suitable and intended for; in fact, all the detail of all drawings should be examined most carefully, to know that they are exact representations of the goods, with a suggestion as to their uses, and that the effect is pleasing and attractive.

The finished cuts soon follow, with proofs of the same. These proofs should be clear and distinct. The illustrations assist in selling the goods, are a necessary expense, and must do justice to the goods. Copy, when handed in from department managers to catalogue department, should be accompanied with all the cuts to be used. Each cut should be numbered and its corresponding number should appear in the copy where the cut is intended to go, and, where possible, all goods should be numbered, to facilitate ordering, care being exercised that no numbers are duplicated. The copy, as submitted, must all be carefully read by the catalogue manager, all cuts examined and compared as to numbers, etc., to see that none are missing and that all appear in their proper places ; anything not satisfactory must be explained, the grammatical construction should be carefully watched, and he is expected to satisfy himself fully that everything about the copy is positively O. K. before passing it. A complete record should be kept of the number of pages of copy handed in from each department, and the number of cuts received, together with date. Also when copy and cuts are given to printer, and when and what proofs are returned from printer and given back to the several departments, as, where copy and proofs are passing through so many different hands at different times, a constant check should be kept on it.

The copy and cuts, when submitted and passed, are handed over to the printer, an effort being made to get them in his hands in the order they should appear in the catalogue, which greatly facilitates his work in many ways, and materially assists in getting the whole catalogue completed much more quickly. Proofs of the catalogue, as set up, are very carefully examined, the arrangement of matter and cuts given special attention, and when every page is entirely satisfactory it is finally O. K.'d. Electrotype or stereotype plates are then made from the type, and these plates handed over to the pressroom, when the work of printing begins. As fast as possible, the forms are printed, folded, gathered and stitched, covers put on, books trimmed and completed.

Special attention is given to preparation of index; every page is gone over carefully, and, as far as possible, every line of goods appearing in the catalogue is alphabetically arranged in the index, thus providing an easy reference to whatever goods customers may wish to select.

Certain space in catalogue is devoted to giving instructions to shoppers by mail, and too much care cannot be exercised in their preparation. They should be short, but cover the ground completely, giving customers whatever information they need to order intelligently, anticipating all contingencies, thus preventing delay, misunderstanding and inconvenience. People are forgetful, and this information, if referred to, acts as a constant reminder. The special points emphasized to customers are—to always write their name, post office, and State or Province, state how much money is enclosed, how and where they want goods shipped, and, if goods are ordered by mail, to enclose sufficient extra for postage and, where necessary, for insurance or registration. They are requested to send remittances by express order, post office order, or other safe means, and cautioned against sending by unregistered mail; to order by number and page in catalogue, and, when requesting samples sent, to state definitely what is required, color, quality, price, etc., so that a suitable selection may be forwarded. Where goods for any reason are returned, they are specially reminded to put their name on the parcel, so that it may be identified at once. They are encouraged to order by freight where possible, to economize on the charges, and to club together with other customers in ordering, for the same reason. They are told definitely what to do in case of delays, complaints or exchanges, and sufficient information is given and classified in such a manner that, if referred to and made use of as intended, there is very little liability of any serious difficulty arising. It wont do to take it for granted that customers always understand what to do. They must be reminded of certain requirements under certain conditions, and largely educated in this direction, and, therefore, instructions to shoppers by mail bear no unimportant relation to the business, and must always be clear, intelligent and complete.

The general arrangement of the catalogue should be studied, with a view to having departments of a similar character grouped together, thus assisting in the general effect.

Economy of space should be studied on every page. While cuts should, as far as possible, be of uniform size, yet they must be no larger than actually necessary to show goods properly, as space occupied by cuts larger than are needed is money wasted. Position and arrangement of cuts can be so studied as to greatly reduce the cost of space. Printed matter must be set close to cuts, and while type selected must be clear and easy to read, yet it must not be large. An understanding should exist with the printer that the matter must be set to save space wherever consistent, and any carelessness or neglect in this respect should be observed and effectually stopped at once. A saving of five pages in a catalogue by watching the size of cuts, their arrangement, the setting of the type, etc., if the issue should be say two hundred thousand, means a million pages of paper saved, outside of any saving in composition, presswork, etc. Such arrangements should be made with the printers as will insure good work throughout. The good effect desired in the special care exercised in preparation of copy, getting drawings and cuts made, etc., can be largely reduced by hasty and careless composition, poor ink, and lack of proper attention to presswork and binding. The printer, therefore, should be wisely selected, one in whom confidence can be placed, who knows how to set it up in the way it will look well, and will use his knowledge so that the catalogue, as representative of the business, will be satisfactory in this particular.

While the catalogue is being compiled and printed, catalogue wrappers are being addressed to customers, and everything prepared for mailing. The method of recording and permanently preserving customers' names and addresses is deserving of attention here. That most in vogue is a system of card indexing. The different towns in each State or Province are written or printed on cards, and these are arranged alphabetically in suitable cases, and ruled so as to show by months and years the amount of business done in each town, and any other particulars required. The name of each customer in the various towns is entered on a separate record card, which is ruled, allowing space for the name and address, and so the date and amount of each purchase is shown as it occurs, space being left at the bottom of each column for total footings, and these individual cards are filed under the town they belong to. Where the towns have a large population and the number of customers is correspondingly large, an auxiliary alphabetical index is used for easy reference. The information recorded on these cards may be entered direct from the orders themselves, or where the loose-leaf book system is used, the sheets may be detached as required, and the information registered direct from these sheets. Each drawer or compartment in which cards are filed is labelled on the outside, to indicate its contents. Thus, when recording an order, the first reference is to the town the order is from, and then under this town is found the card with customer's name, upon which entry is made, and the card put back in its proper place. These cards, therefore, show at all times the name and address of each customer, how much business each has done, and the total amount of business done in each town. Previous to sending out catalogues, these cards are all gone over carefully, and where customers have not ordered within a certain time their cards are taken out. Where two or more names in the same town, and evidently of the same family, appear, positive information is obtained and acted upon, with a view to preventing a waste of catalogues by sending more than one to the same family. The list is thoroughly examined, checked, revised, and all old, dead matter excluded before addressing catalogue wrappers, as sending out catalogues to names that do not respond is a dead loss of postage, printed matter and effort. A big advantage in keeping a mailing list on index cards is, that they can be distributed among a large number of writers, and thousands of wrappers written in a short time, which cannot be conveniently done where kept in books; and the card system also keeps the list neat and clean, while books, by reason of names being crossed out, etc., always present anything but a good appearance. When wrappers are addressed, they are all checked back and compared with cards, to insure absolute correctness. All the wrappers for one town are usually attached together and kept separate from other towns, and thus, when mailing, all the catalogues going to any one town are put in a bag or bags by themselves, which, while causing extra labor on the part of the sender, insures correctness, and enables post office employees to handle large quantities with great despatch. Printed envelopes bearing the firm's name and address, and blank order forms, are usually enclosed for the benefit of the customers.

The art of catalogue compiling and looking after its proper distribution entails hard and extremely careful work. When finished and sent out, it has to compete with other catalogues wherever it goes, and, as it is the representative of the business, it must be complete in every detail, in order to do its work well.

While the catalogue has its distinctive place as "The Steady Trade Bringer" from out-of-town customers, yet much is accomplished by special mail-order advertising. This embraces booklets, circulars, leaflets, etc.; little pamphlets properly illustrated and well written dropped into the people's homes through the medium of the letter, the parcel, or both. Suggestions of seasonable goods, a special about furs when the weather is cold, rubbers and waterproofs during the rainy season, hints for weddings in June, light clothing for warm-weather wear, and so on through the whole range of merchandise, keeping the business before the public all the time with something new, attractive, seasonable. Where "Special Sales" are inaugurated, such as "White Goods Sale," "Special Furniture Sale," etc., shoppers from out of town are given an opportunity to participate in any advantages they may bring through the medium of the newspaper advertisement as far as it reaches, and through such special distribution of advertising matter relative to these sales as is consistent with anticipated profits. The Christmas season is specially considered, the gift question in all its bearings duly studied, planned and provided for in advance. Tuning the business up all the time, keeping at a safe distance any danger of a relapse or "that tired feeling," which may almost unsuspectingly creep into a business, by administering these special advertising tonics, new, interesting and helpful, the result of well-studied plans.

This process of continual construction is not built up alone by keeping in constant touch with customers already secured, but by reaching out for new trade among new people. Getting new names. Regular customers, on request, readily contribute the names and addresses of possible customers in their immediate vicinity. Special appeals made to special classes, for a consideration, usually result in securing satisfactory lists. These lists as received are compared with names already in use, and all duplicates struck out, thus providing against the possibility of sending the same matter to the same name twice. Securing these new names is simply a part of the natural development of the catalogue trade. Wisely considered, the development is both from within and from without. From within, by adding new stocks to the business from time to time, as space, resources and abilities permit; and from without, by adding new and increased numbers to the purchasing list. From within, by getting more goods to sell; and from without, by getting more people to buy. Not only continuing to sell the same goods to the same people, but getting more goods for these same people, and more people to buy these goods. Instead of having the *dollar* sent to some other business for lack of goods, get that *dollar* by having the goods, the effort being made to build up the business and develop it on the lines of selling all the people all their goods

all the time. It is the understanding
of this principle and its working out
through the catalogue and all other
auxiliary advertising, backed up by the
goods required, that makes the possibilities of this trade.

Receiving and Opening Mail.

While the catalogue is under course of construction, the whole mail-order system should be thoroughly gone over, tightened up, well oiled, improved where possible, and put in proper shape to handle the large volume of business which is bound to come immediately after the distribution of catalogues.

Where the mail is large, it is usually brought from the post office by wagon, the smaller deliveries being brought by regular post office carriers. All registered letters and parcels are carefully checked as to number, by actual count, and compared with number entered on post office registration sheets, before signing for them. Envelopes are first cut open by one or more persons. Registered letters are kept separate from all others, are distributed separately and accounted for before any ordinary mail is handled. Each opener is held responsible for the number of letters received, which are checked back, totalled, and the totals must agree with the total number given out by the one in charge. In the event of any error, it must be examined into at once and everything made O. K. A positive check is kept upon all letters and every precaution exercised to prevent the possibility of mistakes or loss of any kind. Ordinary unregistered letters are treated in the same careful manner. Special tables are provided for mail openers, and each one occupies a separate space or division. When a letter is opened, the amount enclosed (whether in bills, express orders, drafts, checks, post office orders, stamps or silver) is carefully counted, checked and entered on the order, totalled and compared with the amount customer claims to have enclosed. If these agree, the amount is signed for by the opener or stamped with an initial stamp, and the envelope is also initialed. The money is usually placed directly on the order it belongs to, both are put in a box or basket specially provided for the purpose, and each succeeding letter, with the remittance it contains, follows in its regular order as opened, until the mail is all completed. In some cases the money and orders are separated at once. Each letter or order is examined carefully, to see that the name and address are given, and if not, the envelope should be attached for reference. If any samples referring to orders are enclosed, they must be attached to the order, and care exercised in attaching measurement forms, plans, or any separate sheets bearing any relation to the order. Should there be any difference in the amount received and the amount customer claims to have enclosed, the attention of the one in charge must be called to it at once, and, after thorough examination, be certified to by one or more. Any omission of samples or enclosures of any kind, or any irregularities of any character, must be reported immediately, examined into, and certified to by those of recognized authority. Ordinary mail, such as enquiries, requests for samples, etc., and all letters not containing money, are kept separate from letters with money enclosed. Orders and money are collected, and the cashier checks and counts all money over again, comparing it with the amount entered on each order by the opener, and, where O. K., stamps each order and envelope with a duplicate consecutive numbering and date stamp. Thus, at almost the first stage of handling an order, it receives its individual number, which is different from the number appearing on any other order, and is used to identify it through the different stages it may have to pass while being completed. Envelopes are separated from orders, and each checker's envelopes put in a package by themselves for reference. Should one be needed, the order is first examined, and, as it bears the checker's signature, reference is then made to

that checker's package of envelopes,
and the one bearing the same number
as the order is easily and quickly found.

Book-keeping, Buying, Checking, Etc.

Where the business is large, the country is usually divided up into districts or sections, each division being designated by a letter; thus one State or Province would be known as "A," and another as "B," and these sections each usually have a head under the supervision of the Manager. A simple form of cash book is largely made use of, by which the number and amount of each order only is entered under its proper division column. The totals of these columns must agree with the total amount of cash received. Orders follow in their natural course to the book-keepers, who, under the date received, enter the orders in regular order by number, name and address, and credit the customer with the amount received. Cashier and book-keepers are able to compare entries by number and amount, and should always agree. All orders, after being entered in the books, are generally examined by one or more appointed for this work, who note anything of importance on the order, marking it in such a manner as to attract special attention. Bargains on sale that day, which are usually marked "Rush," requests to have goods delivered by a certain time, enclosed with a shipment made by another house, or with goods already bought and holding; in fact, anything and everything requiring any particular or extra care, so that no omission of instructions will occur, and that the detail of each order shall be distinctly carried out. All requests for samples, catalogues, etc., are put in hand at once, so that this work is being done promptly, and while the other work in connection with the order is being carried on. All orders, after being examined, everything noted and all specials sorted out, are classified into large, small or medium. All orders for only one article, such as gloves, drugs, jewelry, books, etc., are separated from orders for miscellaneous merchandise, all credits referred to looked up, and everything put into complete shape for buyers to handle. As orders are distributed among the buyers, they are charged with the number received, and are individually held responsible for all orders while in their possession. In some cases buyers are not used, but orders are copied on requisition sheets, and sent to the different departments to be filled; but where a large retail business is done, the method of using buyers is largely adopted. The buyers' duties are many, and a great deal depends upon their ability and skill. They are expected to keep a record of all orders received and how disposed of. Their orders must be read carefully and thoroughly understood; if they lack any information, such as color, size, samples, or any errors in extensions or additions, they must be observed, and, where necessary, consulted about. All requests for estimates or prices asked for on orders

must be got from the proper department, written up clearly, and have
the signature of one whose authority
is recognized. Where goods are going
by express or freight, the buyers
usually make use of a purchasing
card. They are provided with check
books, and, as they visit the different
departments and make their selections,
they make out a check in duplicate for
each purchase, leaving both with the
salesperson. The top check is sent
with the goods to the mail-order
sorting section, and the duplicate is
sent to the cash office, just the same
as though it were actual money. This
duplicate check represents so much
money and is taken in payment for
goods. Great care is exercised in
making out these checks. Not only
is one half treated as cash, but the
other half goes with the goods direct
to the customers, showing them exactly how their money has been
spent. These checks must be written
plainly with good figures, and give a
full description of goods, prices, etc.

The date, exact time purchase is made, the department bought from, sales number and order number, must all appear on each check, and all have such important relations to the work that any omission or carelessness cannot be allowed. On their purchasing card they enter the number of the order they are buying, and enter this same number on every check belonging to that order, also entering each purchase as bought on the purchasing card by department, sales number, and amount. When the purchase is completed, the order and purchasing card are handed to a shipping clerk, who examines the order as to shipping instructions, enters the name and address and how goods are to be shipped on this card, when they are passed to a clerk who examines the order carefully, to see that everything has been bought correctly, no omissions made, all additions correct, and who, when satisfied that the order is executed properly in every particular, sends the order with proper charge slip attached back to the book-keeper, and the purchasing card is sent to the sorting or inspecting room, where goods in the meantime have been sent

Assembling and Packing Mail-Order Goods.

This assembling section is arranged to provide space for goods until each order is completed. Under a system largely made use of by several houses, the original number stamped on the order and entered by the buyer on every check belonging to that order is here made use of as the sorting number. Sorting tables are arranged for receiving goods, and are numbered from one to ten. Checks accompany all goods, and if the number of the check is say 2,617, the goods are placed on No. 7 table; if check is number 2,618, goods would be placed on No. 8 table, and so on. The last figure on every check denotes the table it is to be placed on, and, as orders are numbered consecutively as they are received, the goods are very evenly distributed over the ten tables; and, as all numbers must end in some figure between one and ten, the ten tables thus provide for all numbers.

Shelving is partitioned off back of these tables with a space of about eighteen inches square in each compartment. These compartments are four or more high and as many in number as the business demands. While the last figure in any check number denotes the table it is to be placed on, so the last two figures are made use of to indicate what particular compartment the goods are to be placed in. Thus, check No. 2,617 and goods go to No. 7 table, and when placed go to No. 17 compartment; No. 2,627 with goods go to No. 7 table and No. 27 compartment, and so on, sufficient space being provided for the repetition of these endings as required. No. 2,617 being entered on checks belonging to Mr. Blank's order, and this number appearing on his checks only, all his goods find their way to No. 7 table, and are placed in No. 17 compartment, and checks are filed in this compartment as goods are placed. The purchasing card used by the buyer, and on which the order number and all the items bought appear, is carefully compared with checks, and when checks representing all goods on this card are received the order is complete and ready for packing. All goods as received on sorting tables are opened up, looked over carefully, checked, weighed, measured, colors, sizes, qualities and quantities critically examined, compared with description, and particulars given on checks; and if not satisfactory must be set aside and refused until made O. K. When an order is complete, the goods and card are taken from this inspecting section and sent to the express or freight-packing section of the shipping room, each lot of goods being kept in a separate compartment until packed. Experienced packers are employed, who again, and finally, compare goods with bills, and check everything carefully while packing. According to the nature of the goods, they are wrapped in paper, boxed, baled or crated, entered up in shipping books according to shipping instructions on card, and handed over to the different transportation companies as called for, and cards are filed for reference.

Goods Sent by Mail, Correspondence, Paying for Goods, Etc.

Where goods are ordered to go by mail, checks are made out as before, but with this usual difference, that buyers retain the top check and bring the goods with them. Each item as bought is entered by department, sales number and amount on a shipping and charge sheet. When an order going by mail is all bought, it is carefully checked by the buyer, weighed, and the amount of postage determined as near as possible, when goods and order are handed to shipping clerk, who enters the name and address on the shipping slip, when all are passed to the mailing section, where goods are carefully checked, wrapped, weighed, amount of postage determined, parcels addressed, stamps put on, entered by name, address and amount of postage in a parcel-mailing book, and placed on sorting table, after which they are sorted and placed into different bags by State, Province, or whatever division of parcels the post office authorities may name, that will facilitate rapid handling and quick despatch. Should a parcel, when wrapped, require more postage than customer has allowed money for, it should be laid aside, and the head of division should determine whether to hold parcel and write for the additional amount required, omit something from the parcel, or allow the customer to remit the balance due. Where small amounts are to be returned to customers, in some cases their particular parcels, as wrapped, may be left open at one end and placed on a separate table, where, after checking, a small envelope containing the amount to be returned may be enclosed in the parcel. These little envelopes may be prepared in advance and placed in separate divisions, all one-cent envelopes being in one space, all two-cent envelopes in another, and so on, so that the work can be done rapidly, and a great saving effected in postage on letters which otherwise would require to be written in order to return the balance due. All registered parcels are kept separate and signed for by the post office authorities. It is easy at any time, by reference, to find out exactly how a package was addressed, how much postage was put on the parcel, how much money was enclosed, whether registered or not, and just what mail it was sent out on.

All orders, when properly checked, should be passed back to the book-keepers, who, having made the original entry and credited the cash when the order was first received and before goods were bought, may now refer to that order number, name and address again, and charge the customer with amount of goods sent, amount of postage paid, and cash returned, or remaining to be returned, thus balancing the account. A simple index system may be made use of for any debit or credit balances that may require to be kept. Orders pass on to heads of divisions, who examine all carefully, sorting out any that may be replied to by form cards or letters, seeing that all necessary explanations and enquiries have been submitted, made and signed by those authorized, and that they are satisfactory, and who dictates all necessary replies. All replies, when dictated and type-written, are handed back for examination, and, when correct, are signed and given to cashier, who encloses any balance to be returned, keeping a record of the same by number and amount, when the letters are sent to the mailing section, stamped and mailed, and orders sent to be filed with copy of reply attached.

The graphophone system of dictating and reproducing is largely made use of in place of shorthand where the business is large, and is found to greatly facilitate the handling of correspondence.

Personal representation of the customers by everyone associated with the different departments is especially encouraged. The buyer who visits the departments cannot be compelled to accept anything except what in her judgment is O. K. She represents the customers absolutely, stands in their place, and studies their interests at every turn, and this same personal interest is specially observed by every individual clerk in whatever relation they may bear to orders or goods passing through their hands.

The payment for goods purchased by the mail-order department is extremely simple. The duplicate checks made out by buyers and given to salespeople when selecting goods represent so much money, and are sent to the cash office immediately. They are collected here and sent to the check office or auditing department daily, where they are all audited. The total amount of these checks represents the total amount of goods bought that day, and the mail-order cashier thus hands over the exact amount required to pay for goods received. As these checks also show the different departments goods have been purchased from, they are all sorted out by departments, and each department, therefore, receives credit for its share of the money.

Likewise is it easy to know at all times just what percentage of cost the total mail-order expense is upon the business done. The mail order expense properly consists of its share of light, heat, power and rental, sundry expenses, such as stationery, office fixtures, furniture and wages paid. The wages list, properly divided, should show how much is paid for buying, book-keeping, type-writing, samples, checking, packing, etc., and if wages paid in each division week by week and the amount of business done are compared with any previous week's expenses and business, the department is promptly made aware of any unnecessary increased expense, just exactly where that unnecessary increase is, and the remedy may be applied at once. The catalogue expense may also be readily arrived at. The total issue costs a certain amount, and according to the number of pages each department occupies, so in this proportion may be estimated each one's share in the expense. Each department manager, knowing what his catalogue space may have cost for a certain issue, and what amount of business he may have done from that issue, can estimate exactly what percentage of cost his mail-order advertising is upon his sales, while the total catalogue expense for any one issue may be added to the other total mail-order expense for that time, and the exact percentage of cost may be arrived at upon the total amount of mail-order business done. Such a system may be adopted and made actual use of that will point out at once the exact condition of every part of this business, and provide a safety valve which will indicate at all times the true profit or loss, and through just what channel that loss or gain accrues.

Filing Correspondence.

Systems of filing differ, but where the business is large, one of two methods is largely adopted, that is filing either by number or place.

When filed by number, the original number stamped on the order is made use of for filing purposes.

Where the place file is used, suitable boxes or drawers are arranged in cases, each box being labelled on the outside indicating its contents. These drawers are provided with cards on which are printed or written the different post offices in each State or Province, and arranged for easy reference. Thus all correspondence coming from any one town is filed together next its town card, and where the mail from any one town is large it may be subdivided by an alphabetical index. Thus, to find Mr. B.'s order from Blank Town reference is first made to the drawer which contains Blank Town, and under this town, among the Bs, will be found

Mr. B.'s orders. One set of drawers may be made use of for each month's filing, and, therefore, as many sets of drawers are provided as will correspond with the number of months letters may be preserved. Separate files may also be kept (usually alphabetical by name) for filing letters, such as those where customers have forgotten to give size, color, or measurements, where they have overlooked enclosing samples, or any omission or circumstance which may cause customers to be written to and their orders held for further information, or orders that may have any balance holding to credit, etc.

The filing must be very accurately done, as constant reference is made, and it is of the utmost importance that any correspondence required shall be found with the greatest despatch.

Special Orders.

A special effort should be made to have the system so arranged that it will enable the mail-order department, as well as every other department in connection with the house, to know how many orders are partly bought and holding for goods which have been ordered that are not in stock, or that require to be made. The buyer who finds anything asked for on an order which a department cannot supply at once (and no checks should be taken unless the order can be filled promptly) should give someone appointed by each department full particulars of what is required, the number of the order, name of customer, description, size, or measurements of goods to be made or procured. When everything is bought, with these exceptions, the order should be then handed to a special mail-order clerk, who should note what is lacking to complete the order, and in a set of special department files (space being provided for each department) should place the holding order. He should visit the different departments, ascertaining particulars concerning each order, find out what efforts are being made to fill the same, and crowd these orders to completion, where necessary, writing customers explaining any cause of delay. As each department secures the goods required, the mail order department should be notified immediately, when the order may be quickly produced from its department file, check made out and order completed. It is easy to ascertain at any time through such a system exactly what goods each department lacks, and direct such efforts as will provide for the least possible lack of stock and the least possible delay in executing orders.

Returned Goods, Exchanges, and Complaints.

A separate section should be devoted to returned goods or exchanges. As goods are received the packages should be examined as to identification, whom and where from, and entered up alphabetically under the date received, with all particulars required, and goods placed in suitable compartments. When letter of explanation is received, goods are easily located, and both should be given to special exchange clerks, who will secure the necessary exchange bills and make such new selections as customers may desire.

The cause of all goods returned should be thoroughly investigated in every instance, and where the fault lies with the house, the customer should be reimbursed for any extra expense incurred; and whatever department or individual is to blame should be made fully acquainted with their error, and such steps taken as will prevent a repetition of it.

Usually associated with this work is a special section, which should deal with all letters of complaint. The cause of all complaints should be fully enquired into and at once. There should be no delay whatever, but immediate answers insisted upon. Explanations should be complete and to the entire satisfaction of customers, and any loss through carelessness or errors made good without reserve. Each department and their help should be held strictly accountable for any claims which, upon investigation, show where the responsibility should rest. This feature of promptly adjusting all differences and satisfying every reasonable demand leads to continued and increased confidence, and should, therefore, be given very particular attention.

Samples.

The preparation, selection and sending out of samples should receive the most careful attention. In some cases requests for samples are distributed among the different departments and are filled and sent to the sample department, but this method with progressive houses is considered slow, and for this reason alone unsatisfactory.

The improved method is to cut from the piece such lengths of goods as are required. These are sent to the sample department with width, price and full particulars, where suitable paper printed in squares, the size of sample to be sent, are attached. These are sewn by machines driven by electric power and afterwards cut in proper sizes by electric cutting knife, prices inserted and placed in partitioned spaces in drawers arranged in suitable cabinets. As requests for samples are received, they are filled direct from these drawers, and sent out by the next mail. Help is employed here who by long experience become familiar with all classes of sampleable goods, and who are under the direct management of one who thoroughly understands interpreting the customers' wants, and who bears no unimportant part to whatever measure of success may result from the sale of all goods by sample.

Keeping Employees' Time.

This position requires a man of considerable firmness, as he comes in contact with every employee, and is bound to enforce the discipline of the house as applied to absentees and lates, regardless of any partiality or favoritism. He has direct charge of the cloakrooms, and must see that they are kept neat and clean, and that each individual has a certain space allotted. He should be on duty early and late, and should see that every one registers their time in passing in and out. A record of all employees going out on passes should be kept, and none should be accepted unless signed by those authorized. He should keep a record of employees' names and addresses, and have the same checked up regularly. He should supply wages department and also heads of departments with a report of all who are absent. Where so many are under the charge of heads of departments, it is impossible for them to tell at once who may be absent. The time-keeper should notify them promptly every morning and noon, and they will thus be enabled to arrange immediately, so that the work done by absentees is provided for. He should not allow parcels of any kind to be carried in or out of the store, nor allow anyone to reënter the store after passing the time desk in going out, or return to the cloakrooms after passing the time desk going in.

As part of the store help must go to dinner at one hour and part at another, he should regulate it so that those who go out one hour are back in their departments before others are notified, thus preventing crowding on stairways and passages. Departments are usually notified by bells, and each is familiar with its particular signal. Doors should be closed sharp on the minute, and all lates excluded. No matter what system for registering time is used, it is easy to determine who is late or absent, as on coming in all keys or time cards hanging on the time board are on one side of the time clock, and when the time is registered they are hung on the opposite side. Those which have not been removed indicate at once who has not come in. Time cards of any absent, who have not sent in a reason for absence, should be removed from the time board and such employees should secure permission from those authorized before their time can be again marked. Lists of those going on holidays should be supplied time-keeper, and their cards should also be removed. The time-keeper should supply the wages department with correct time sheets, as desired. He should see that employees are orderly in passing in and out, and permit no loitering in the cloakrooms. A register is usually placed at the exit door, which should be signed by one appointed for each department or section of the store when leaving at night, certifying that all persons have left their department, and that all windows are secured, blinds down, etc.

Employing Help.

The hiring of help is largely centered in one individual for the entire store. Departments requiring additional help should notify the employment office, and give particulars of the kind of help required, which fact should be noted and filed for reference, a preference being given former employees seeking reëngagement. The hours for engaging help are usually from 8 to 10 A. M., after which no applications are considered for that day. All applicants must be treated with courtesy. Even though no immediate help is required, applicants in many cases are permitted to fill out application, which should be placed on file for reference, and a satisfactory applicant may then be notified as soon as a position is open. All applications should contain, as far as possible, full particulars concerning applicant. It should show the date of engagement, name, address, whether married or single, nationality, church denomination, where previously employed, for how long, and reasons for leaving. References should be given, who may be communicated with, and whose replies should be attached to application. Application blank should show salary agreed upon and for what particular department employed. Space should be provided for percentage record, and for transfer from one department to another, for increased salary recommendations, which are usually signed by heads of departments and passed by those appointed. They should be at all times a complete and permanent record of each employee. All help is usually engaged upon the distinct understanding and agreement that they are privileged to leave any day, or their services may be dispensed with at any time. A new employee, when given a time card or key, and the timekeeper has explained the system of registering time, etc., and allotted cloakroom space, is conducted to the head of the department or assistant.

Paying Wages.

The system of registering time furnishes accurate information for estimating wages. The time sheets kept by the time-keeper are here made use of. The name of each employee under the respective department each one is attached to, with number, rate of wages per week, number of days worked, actual wages due, etc., should be entered on the wages sheet. The total amount of money required on any pay day is given wages office, each individual's pay is placed in a pay envelope, sealed, numbered and entered in signature book. Each head of a department, or one appointed, receives all wages for that department, signing for the same, and sees that they are distributed and signed for by each individual as received. The work is done accurately and with despatch, as thousands are by this method paid their weekly earnings in a very short time.

Watchmen.

Watchmen should report at the store each night, and as soon as the store is closed examine the leaving register, to see that each department has signed for everything having been left in perfect order. They should examine at once all doors and windows, seeing that they are securely fastened; also all other entrances to building, and all places where anyone might be concealed. They should report in writing anything irregular occurring during the night, leaving the same at the office, and repeat the report until the irregularity has been attended to. A regular patrol should be made throughout the entire building. An ingenious system of clock registration is made use of in some cases, which indicates upon examination in the morning the different stations each watchman has passed and the exact time of each passing during the entire night. In the event of fire or any other accident occurring

during the night, such special instructions should be followed as will meet
with the ready response of whatever
assistance may be required.

General Rules for Employees.

Rules for employees are in force in all large Department Stores. Different stores differ in detail of rules, but the application is the same, all serving to build up the system of government which directs and controls the entire management. Weekly examinations are held in some instances, and familiarity with the rules exacted, thus enforcing and maintaining system and discipline.

The hours for opening and closing business vary at different seasons of the year, of which due notice is given. The opening hour is usually 8 o'clock, at which time all employees are expected to be in their respective positions, all covers folded and put in proper places, stocks and counters dusted, and everything made ready for the day's business.

All employees must enter and leave the store by employees' entrance, leaving all wraps, hats, rubbers, lunches, etc., in the cloakroom, which is conveniently arranged for this purpose.

Upon entering the store in the morning and upon leaving and returning at noon, and on going out at night, each individual records his or her time. If for good reason an employee is necessarily delayed, a permission pass may be obtained to commence work; but if late without a good reason being given, they cannot commence work until noon, and thus lose a half day's work and a half day's pay. Attendance to business must be punctual and regular. Continued lateness and absence would merit discharge.

Employees who are absent for any cause must notify the house at once, either the head of their department or time-keeper, and satisfactory reasons given for being absent.

Whenever a change of address is made, employees must report same to time-keeper at once.

Employees must never leave the store during business hours (except for dinner) without a pass signed by the head of the department and countersigned by one authorized. Blank pass books are usually supplied heads of departments. These passes should give the names of employees, their numbers, what departments employed in, date and time of going out, and must be presented to the time-keeper, who will permit employees to go to the cloakroom for wraps and pass them out.

Employees must not leave their departments to go to any other part of the store without informing the head of the department, or assistant, and obtaining permission.

Employees desiring to purchase goods for themselves are expected to do so during the least busy hours, usually from 8 to 9 A. M. A pass to purchase must be obtained from the head of the department. This pass is exchanged for a purchasing card. All employees' purchases must be made on purchasing card and sent by the regular delivery. If for any reason a parcel cannot be sent by the regular delivery, and employee is to carry it home, these parcels must be O. K.'d by the proper party. A numbered check is given to the employee and a duplicate attached to the parcel. By presenting this check at the exit door, the package is delivered to the proper party. Parcels are not allowed to be carried into the store by employees. The wagons call upon request and deliver packages to the parcel office, where they may be obtained.

Employees are to avoid gossiping and not allow their time to be taken up with friends who desire to visit with them during business hours. Loud conversation to be avoided.

Business hours not to be occupied in reading books, papers, letter writing, needlework, etc. Loafing or wasting time away from departments not allowed.

Extravagance and display in dress to be avoided. The use of striking colors and patterns is objectionable. The costume should be modest and neat in appearance.

Employees are expected to be courteous to each other, using the same dignity, respect, and care in addressing others that they feel they are entitled to themselves.

Should clerks be deserving of censure, it should be done in a gentlemanly manner, not before other employees or customers, thus retaining the respect of each other.

The use of gum or tobacco, eating nuts, fruits, candy, or lunches during business hours is strongly objected to. Loitering around the outside of the building, on the corners or at the entrances, expectorating on the walks and giving the premises an untidy appearance will not be permitted. Defacing the walls, counters or fixtures, or abusing the property in any way, means immediate dismissal.

All employees must learn to obey the orders of those whose authority is recognized, and be governed by the rules and regulations of the house; not only because they must, but for their own individual interests, and the interests of the house in general. Some rules may appear rigid, but they are deemed necessary, and, therefore, must be obeyed, and the living up to them is not intended to be a reflection on the self-respect of any one.

Mechanical Section.

Underneath the selling space in these large stores lies the network of machinery, all necessary for the prompt and careful adjustment of each day's work, furnishing the power for heating, lighting, elevator service, etc. Modern automatic sprinkler system always ready for an emergency, rendering the property and merchandise as nearly fireproof as possible, aided by a corps of properly-drilled firemen taken from the regular employees staff. Pneumatic cash system connecting with every part of the store selling space ; not only utilized for carrying cash, but also providing the means of ventilation, by using up and discharging thousands of cubic feet of impure air regularly, and bringing fresh air into the building constantly. Complete staffs of engineers, carpenters, painters, etc., are almost constantly employed in looking after additions, alterations, and repairs, thus keeping the whole

building in perfect condition. All
are under the direct management of
experts, whose mechanical skill is
utilized to assist in rendering the
store service complete, and whose
services are recognised on an equality
with those occupying the most responsible positions in connection with
the business.